DIG ANOTHER WELL

Go ahead; dig up God's blessing for your career.

Wait, hold up….!

***If this little book helps you,
let us know your thoughts.***

e-mail:* *prestojob@gmail.com

- Or -

Text: 727-458-2690

Copyright 2019 Robert Meier

Lightspeed Press
www.fastrackjobs.org
prestojob@gmail.com
Phone: 727-998-6169

Cover Design Marisa Meier

Library of Congress Cataloging-in Publication Data on file with publisher.
ISBN:0-9744483-6-2

Printed in the United States
First printing 2010

TABLE OF CONTENTS

SECTION	Page

INTRODUCTION

"Red Bull Gives You Wings" is a brilliant slogan that most Americans have heard many times due to the ubiquitous TV advertising the company uses to sell their now famous energy drink in the ultra-competitive beverage market. Although it's easy for us to scoff at the promise of a burst of energy flowing from yellowish taurine juice, the fact that three billion cans were sold in 2006 alone indicates that there are millions of people who crave the jolt the slogan promises. I mention Red Bull as way of introduction to *Dig Another Well* because in some ways it captures the essence of what I want to do; provide a spiritual lift to those who are growing weary as they search for a new job.

Whereas the compassionate side of me does sympathize with weary job seekers who are struggling to continue hunting for a job that pays a livable wage, the career coach in me knows that a job search is war. In war, you toughen your troops and strengthen their resolve for the battle ahead.

Now any general who has had to marshal troops onto the battlefield knows the insidious erosion of morale, confidence and motivation caused by a lengthy war campaign can often do the most harm. Likewise, many job searches often last for months, a cycle of time that can zap our resolve and make us want to give up. Don't do it. Churchill's famous quote applies to you and your search; "We shall never surrender. We shall not flag nor fail, we shall go on to the end." What choices we make in the dark moments of a long job search will determine whether we grasp the hand of victory or crash in discouraged defeat.

PROLOGUE

Some might think that telling others to dig a new well is easier said than done. So please let me start our relationship by sharing how I dug a new well to get this book into your hands.

It started in 2004 when I was invited once again to be a guest on the Christian radio program *Midday Connection*. If you don't know about *Midday Connection*, it is produced by Moody Bible Institute (the Chicago-based church founded by its namesake, Dwight L. Moody) and has been running for over 15 years. It is an hour-long program broadcast live to over 100 radio stations across the U.S. Now I had been on Midday a few times previously sharing tips and tricks on career subjects and, although I was born-again in 1993, I never felt comfortable mixing my career coaching with my faith on a very direct basis. That all changed during the show in 2004.

For a couple of weeks prior to my appointment, I had been talking to my wife Marisa about what the Lord was showing me regarding careers in relationship to Christians. At first it was awkward to verbalize the feeling that our careers, which seemed so opposite to the more spiritual issues of faith and family, was a ground-zero issue to God. It just seemed self-serving to connect careers and belief, a connection I had avoided for over a decade. But this time I couldn't let it go.

Essentially what was on my heart was the idea of how our work should display the glory of God in our lives. But the crux of the problem is that many believers find it impossible to uncover their own luster for presentation to a skeptical job market and therefore miss out on winning great job offers that fits them personally. I wanted to teach listeners how to find employment where their gifts and talents could bloom and where God could use them more greatly for his kingdom's purpose. Imagine, I told Marisa, what could happen if Christians were taught that healthy faith, healthy families and healthy careers are equally important to God? What if believers could learn to stop being afraid to fight for job advancement as they pursue God's destiny for their careers.

> Imagine if believers dug up the jewels of their work accomplishments, polished and displayed them for employers to buy (i.e. hire). The country would have men and women of faith in senior management roles who could posi-

tively impact the ethical, moral and business cultures of their company. It would be a revolution.

Of course the nagging voice in my head told me otherwise. "Aren't you preaching the gospel of prosperity," I started to ask myself? "Don't careers steal parents from their children and their spouses?" "Christians don't need to worry about reaching the CEO's office, they need to learn to be content just where they are." And I began to doubt the vision to use my career coaching expertise to help believers advance professionally. Nevertheless, on that particular Midday Connection I wanted to remind listeners that we were made in God's image and that the image of God is glorious. Therefore we should reflect that glory of God and what better place to do that than where our gifts and talents are on display, which is often where we work. So what's the problem? Well many of us don't feel like jewels and really don't know how to dig up the diamonds in our careers, so essentially we present ourselves on paper (the resume) and in person (the interview) like dirt clods rather than sparkling gems.

During the show I shared a couple simple ways that listeners could dig up their career diamonds, cut the facets in their job histories, polish the luster and set these jewels on display for potential employers to purchase.

The end result was an overwhelming response. Within one hour my website had over 5,000 visitors, which is no small feat because the show host never gave out my website address. In order for 5,000 people to click my URL they had to do the following; 1) Click Moody's Home Page, 2) Click Programs, 3) Click Midday Connection, 4) Click Today's Guest and 5) Click onto my website. And within an hour thousands of believers did just that and thus my burden came alive.

The pursuit of filling God's calling for my life has led me to dig, with the help of my wife and support of my children. May God bless your digging.

Welcome to *Dig Another Well*

When Christians suffer from being fired, downsized, rationalized or made redundant (in this day and age, who hasn't), "Dig Another Well" hopefully will be the story they read that will lift them up, dust them off emotionally as well as the shovel that helps them start digging again.

The story is based on a small set of verses in a single Bible chapter, Genesis Ch. 26, when Isaac journeys from being kicked out of the land where he was prospering professionally (right after his best fiscal year when God increased his holdings a hundredfold) to being forced to seek a new place to earn a living. Of course, he might have seen it coming (the Philistines were jealously capping the wells he used to water his livestock). However, like many who hold onto a job too long, even when the "writing is on the wall," Isaac waited until the ax fell. After he dug four new wells, of which three were fought over, he found peace and a path that led straight to God.

Now why don't we hear from Isaac himself and see how he found encouragement in the midst of tremendous opposition.

13

CHAPTER I

WHEN GOOD TIMES GO BAD, DIG AGAIN

Oh, how I remember what it felt like as if it were just yesterday. But before I begin, please allow me to make your acquaintance; I'm Isaac, son of Abraham. You may not be too familiar with my story, so let me get us all on the same piece of parchment.

> Genesis Chapter 26: verses 12-17; Isaac planted crops in that land and the same year reaped a hundredfold, because the LORD blessed him. The man became rich, and his wealth continued to grow until he became very wealthy. He had so many flocks and herds and servants that the Philistines envied him. So all the wells that his father's servants had dug in the time of his father

Abraham, the Philistines stopped up, filling them with earth. Then Abimelech said to Isaac, "Move away from us; you have become too powerful for us." So Isaac moved away from there and encamped in the Valley of Gerar and settled there.

Of course, that's the fancy way to tell you what happened, I'm here to give you the story straight from the camel's mouth. You may have noticed that I just received a hundredfold blessing from the Lord. Boy, did I have it made. I remember thinking the milk and honey would flow forever. Not that me and Rebekah (my better half) didn't have our share of tough times, mind you, we had moved from Beer Lahai Roi in the first place due to a recession, although we called it a famine in the old days. By the time we reached Gerar, we thought we were planted for life.

I should have seen it coming. The Philistines were pretty jealous and looking for a fight. What I thought was petty bickering over water rights turned into an all out attack on our business model. I could have worked things out fine if they just had the nerve to talk to me directly, but that didn't happen. Nope, just one well after another got plugged up, making life hard for everybody.

Are you wondering why I didn't see the "writing on the wall?" Look, when you see your income increase a hundredfold in a single fiscal year, who's asking questions. Think about it in modern terms. Let's say you earned six figures, or $100,000 last year and this year you see you salary jump 100-fold, that's a heck of a lot of shekels. Matter of fact, do the math; the sum is ten million dollars. I wasn't looking for trouble; I thought everything would work out in the long run. After all, we'd grown fond of the neighborhood, the kids were happy at school and I was well respected around town.

Nevertheless, I wasn't too shocked when king Abimilech dropped by. At least he was diplomatic, making it sound like I had become too successful, his exact words were, "too powerful". He tried to soften the blow with a lot of chitchat about how a young man with my drive, credentials and seasoned abilities would find a new "place to pitch my tent" and get back to climbing the "corporate pyramid" in no time. Then he offered to buy me out with a golden donkey cart, I bet it was just to appease his conscience. You should have heard Rebekah when Abimilech left, did I get an earful. "How could he just push us out of the corner tent like that, what an ingrate!" "Doesn't he know that God's blessing on you, spills over to him?" She did have a good point there. I mean, after all, the Philistines, a rather rowdy bunch, did not have a single war during the time we were there. In addition, I was a big employer, the major mutton supplier, and considering the "Multiplier Effect;" our impact to the local community was immense. Hadn't he ever heard of "Trickle Down Economics?" But that's just what I should have expected from a heathen.

So what is a son of Abraham to do when the local potentate makes a personal house call to let you know you were being "downsized"? We had to make plans to move forward quickly and I got to work on setting our exit strategy immediately.

Reader Takeaway

The result of overstaying your welcome with an employer can lead to stagnation, economic scarcity, and missing other blessings that God wants to give us as we respond to his direction for our career path. If we decide that God has a static will, it is as if we are putting him in a box. Not responding to God's dynamic will for our life, can be compared to what happens when the course of a river changes, but a branch of the river keeps going on its own merry way and doesn't remain fully connected to the main source, the result is a branch filled with stagnate water.

We can become so "rutted" that it takes a shocking jolt to bang us out of our comfort zone. Quite often God gives us an indication that he is moving in a new direction. When it comes to our career for example, indicators can include merger or acquisition rumors that filter down the corporate grapevine, or a new boss who expects long hours of overtime, including Sunday mornings, or a technology that has the potential to make your skills obsolete. These telltale markers can be the "writing on the wall" to let us know that we should consider a new career direction. But hold it, didn't God prosper Isaac wildly in Gerar? Isn't a hundredfold increase in wealth equivalent to going from $100,000 per year to $10 million per year? Why in the world would Isaac think about jumping off the gravy train?

God in his loving kindness wants us to learn to trust him, not our riches. He wants us to respond to him and to act upon his will. Isaac exemplifies the problem of being stuck in a rut, of being shocked out of the rut, and needing to persistently pursue God's will and be ready for a change of plans, even if things seem to be going our way. Change is the essence of faith, which is defined in Hebrews Chapter 11 verse 1, "As the substance of things hoped for, the evidence of things unseen." Faith is really the essence of a job search and according to Hebrews 11, verse 6; without faith it is impossible to please God. God is faithful to direct our path we simply need to respond to his Spirit as it helps us reach his perfect destination.

Illustration – let me introduce you to one of the most amazing clients I have ever served. In this case, someone who started digging a new well as soon as she read the writing on the wall and before the ax finally fell. Cindy Thorsen hired me in 1995 when I still ran a resume service in my four-hundred and fifty dollar a month, one room apartment that ran hard along the Chicago Transit Authority's Red 'L' Line. Not a particularly good place to meet executives but a wonderful place if you are a die-hard Cubs fan. I used to call it the schizophrenic neighborhood; full of yuppies climbing the corporate ladder rushing to get on the 'L' between 7am and 9am, then the walking dead (unemployed, alcoholics and tourists) until the 5PM rush-hour when the yuppies return home. I remember Cindy because she was cutting edge hip, young, rich, confident and very pretty; all blond hair and blue eyes. I also remembered feeling that my 'office' décor, not to mention, location, was quite inadequate for this caliber of client, but that was all I could afford in the mid-90's.

At the time my business name was Absolute Career Services and was found under the resume heading in the Chicago Yellow Pages. I believed the name Absolute was brilliant since the first two letters, A-b seemed to give my expensive display advertisement top billing .

Of course, that was until I saw six of my competitors outsmart me by using the alphabet to their advantage with listings such as AAA Action Resumes and A1 Resumes.

Cindy had called me for a simple resume update that was prompted by the fact that her employer, Chicago & North Western Railway Company, had been recently bought by the giant Union Pacific Railroad. Cindy knew that she didn't want to relocate to Omaha, Nebraska to keep a job that wasn't guaranteed but dangled before her as bait to keep her on during the merger integration. Cindy hired me to start the job search before her termination date, which was 6-week hence.

Now what I failed to mention was that Cindy had had an earlier job search that had left scars and she did not want a repeat of the problem this time. You see, in 1991 Cindy was a newly minted MBA from one of the most prestigious business schools in the country, Northwestern University's Kellogg Graduate School of Management. And like many young MBA grads, Cindy had thought that the degree was her golden ticket to professional success and entitled her to the fast lane to career "easy street." But that is not what happened. Instead she spent six months looking for work, if you don't recall, the early 90's was the middle of a full recession. Even with an Internship at the Nurtrasweet Company, after a half-year of job searching, all she could land was an Associate Media Manager role at Sears National Catalog, and her pay was under $50,000 per year, a far cry from the six-figure job she had expected to land. It is worth remembering; contrary to what the education industry wants you to believe, a good degree does not always equal the promise of a great job.

With the memory of underemployment planted firmly in her mind's eye, once the merger announcement was made she did not hesitate to begin preparing to job-hunt earnestly and hired me to rewrite her resume.

Two interesting facts come out because Cindy took quick initiative. First, when she began to send out her resumes, she was still an employee of C&NW. This is very important, because employers find currently employed job-seekers much more attractive than unemployed. Secondly, because she allowed me to build her a new 'shovel' (resume), she was able to dig her well much faster. The end result for Cindy was multiple job offers within six weeks and the one she accepted gave her a three-title promotional boost to VP of Investor

Relations for a $2.1 billion dollar company, they made her the first female on their executive team, doubled her base salary (with bonus, she actually quadrupled it by the end of the year) and enabled her to change industries into a field she had no previous experience, Real Estate Investment Trusts (REITs). Cindy shows us that quick, proactive response to business change, in her case, an announced merger, led her to a new well without the turmoil associated with waiting too long. By the way, Cindy's career arc led her to become the Senior VP of Investor Relations for the huge technology company called CDW.

CHAPTER II

DAD'S MAP WON'T HELP

Intro - Isaac had just been kicked out of the land where he had prospered greatly and now he must find a new source of sustenance quickly to sustain his family, his servants and his flocks...

Once the king left our tent, I began thinking of relocation options. Now I don't want to make a pyramid out of a sand hill, but it's not easy moving 10,000 cattle, 15,000 sheep, 200 Camels and more than 50 servants – on a day's notice. So you can imagine that I was more than a little distressed with the move. When I finally calmed Rebekah down long enough to discuss our next step, of course her first suggestion was, "What about

27

Egypt? We could move back to Brazenly Hills near the Nile, they have an urbane civilization and your favorite meat pies could be bought by the bushel."

To say I was shocked would be an understatement. I couldn't believe what I was hearing. God had personally told us not to return to Egypt and now my Rebekah, my dear, dear beloved wife was thinking that God would honor our slavish return to a land that was far away physically, and spiritually remote from Him. I had to think fast. An idea started to cross my mind. What if we moved out of town, you know, not too far away maybe to a suburb where we could get out of harm's way? The more I thought about it, the more I liked the idea. My dad Abraham had, years ago, built a thriving business in a nearby suburb, Gerar Valley and I thought I could return and get the business up and running again. Matter of fact, since the only difference in the name was the word Valley, all the worker's uniforms could be easily modified, same with the letterhead and even signage on the chariots. Oh how sweet it is to have a plan that can work.

Off we went to VOG (Valley of Gerar) to find my father's wells, not a simple task. Sand shifts, filled-up wells are not easy to spot in the middle of a desert, and the process of digging seemed to go on forever. Finally, we got the work finished and the flocks watered. We were just beginning to settle down when I got the newest bad news. Now, I don't want you to think I'm making anything up, so let me reference the good book:

> Genesis 26:17-20: So Isaac moved away from there and encamped in the Valley of Gerar and settled there. Isaac reopened the wells that had

been dug in the time of his father Abraham, which the Philistines had stopped up after Abraham died, and he gave them the same names his father had given them. Isaac's servants dug in the valley and discovered a well of fresh water there. But the herdsmen of Gerar quarreled with Isaac's herdsmen and said, "The water is ours!" So he named the well Esek (which means dispute in English).

There you have it, the same old problem all over again. I mean, how greedy are these Philistines? I could understand their jealousy in the city of Gerar, but can't they leave the valley alone, come on, that's unfair. Moreover, I thought going back to restart the family wells would no way encroach upon anyone else's water rights. This reminded me of the old saying, "The best laid plans of scorpions and slaves, often goes awry."

I started to ponder my options. I could stay and fight or I could start a class action suit or I could throw in the towel. Whatever I decided was not going to be popular with Rebekah or easy to implement. I really didn't have enough job skills to be a tent maker, or a money-changer or to start a long haul chariot service. Maybe I was just unlucky. I'm sure there has to be a place big enough for all of us somewhere.

So far I had been kicked out of the place I was thriving and now I had been kicked out of the family business. If I didn't have bad luck, I wouldn't have any luck at all. Just then I remembered the promise that God gave me before we had moved to Gerar in the first place:

> Genesis 26:2-6 The LORD appeared to Isaac and said, "Do not go down to Egypt; live in the

land where I tell you to live. Stay in this land for a while, and I will be with you and will bless you. For to you and your descendants I will give all these lands and will confirm the oath I swore to your father Abraham. I will make your descendants as numerous as the stars in the sky and will give them all these lands, and through your offspring all nations on earth will be blessed, because Abraham obeyed me and kept my requirements, my commands, my decrees and my laws." So Isaac stayed in Gerar.

Well I thought, better stick to my guns and look nearby for God's blessing to return.

Reader Takeaway –

Isaac's situation illustrates a series of events compressed into a few verses in a single chapter of the Bible. Initially Isaac trusted God for his provision in the face of famine (that's why he went to Gerar in the first place) when conventional wisdom might have been to strike his fortune in the bigger metropolis of Egypt. However, that was not God's will for Isaac. So Isaac dutifully goes to Gerar and, sure enough, God blesses him there – perfect, just as planned. Suddenly the blessing turns into a trial, so to speak. Meaning Isaac's hundredfold increase produces jealousy and strife that leads to being kicked out of the land. Not exactly expected by Isaac, but certainly within the realm of possibilities. If you are counting, there is one positive (a hundredfold increase) and one negative (kicked out by Abimlich), so it's a wash.

Since Isaac can't fight an entire kingdom, he takes off to find God's next blessing. At this time he has a deep bank account and doesn't feel too worried about his next step. But, like anybody who has sunk his or her roots deeply in a community, Isaac wants to stay close to his original source of blessing, which in this case is Gerar.

That leads him to choose the Valley of Gerar where he and his servants do the hard work of looking for God's next blessing by digging up the wells of his father Abraham. But instead of finding God's blessing in the old family business, he finds Esek, or quarrel, not good. For those of you who are counting, there are now a total of one blessing and two non-blessings (if we weren't E.C. (evangelically correct), Isaac might call the score, two to one (+1 blessing and –2 curses). Now a little anxiety creeps into Isaac with some confusion to boot. Here we see Isaac trying to stick with God's apparent plan (stay in Gerar) and not stray too far from His will. But all that seems to happen is more problems. You can almost hear him thinking, "I'm willing to give God another chance to prove that he is faithful. After all, I am doing my part. But, does God know the pressure I am under with all my staff, my wife, and my herds? If we don't find water soon we are in big trouble."

We too, often find ourselves doing spiritual calculations; adding up our blessings and subtracting curses to see if God is still on our side. This is a dangerous proposition. If we start to believe that God is <u>not</u> good, to think that God is actually evil, our bond of faith in God can be broken. And this would be a great victory for the enemy of our soul. Once our faith in God is destroyed, then we have a much higher likelihood to drift away from him, from our church and even from those we love.   The question to ask yourself when strife confronts you, "Is God Good?" If you know God's love and have the expectation for eternal life, the answer will be "yes."   The problem is the very next word – but. "Yes, but, doesn't God see our financial need. Yes, but doesn't he see that my husband is stressed out. Yes, but our kids will have to leave their friends." This leads us to ask, "Does God care?" The but... is the gate that allows doubts and fears to pour into our hearts. We can't become defeated by the slew of doubts that follow the "but." The key is to have a child like heart and count our blessings one by one to be amazed by what the Lord has done.

In order to thrive in the face of adversity, you need to know there is purpose and value to trials and that God is eternally faithful. Romans chapter five verses 3-5 tells us, that trials produce persistence and persistence leads to character and character, hope. Think of the persistence Jesus had to posses to go to the cross. The persistence Paul had to have to evangelize in the face of death threats. The persistence of Joseph to believe God when he was in prison, or Daniel when thrown into the lion's den. The Bible is full of examples that we can read for help in times of strife. Remember, God doesn't want us to rest on our laurels or to allow past success to blind us to his future plans. Rather, God's intention is to make our life both a training ground and a personal adventure for every believer.

Illustration – Antonio Passin was named for his Italian great-grandfather who immigrated to America in the early 1900's and founded the iconic Radio Flyer toy wagon company. Antonio, like many children who grow up in the shadow of the family business wanted to see what he could accomplish on his own in the job market. After completing a bachelor's degree in architecture at the University of Kansas and a year-long study in Urban Design at the University of Notre Dame, Antonio took on multiple junior architectural roles as designer and draftsman for various firms. He then spent three years trying to build up his own architectural company with mixed results. Although Antonio worked for some of the better Chicago architects including the well-respected Perkins & Will, his solo architectural career never really took off. So when his family asked for his help to rescue Radio Flyer from obsolescence, Antonio was ready to return and for a couple years, his efforts were quite prosperous. That was before disaster struck and Antonio came to my office to help him dig a new well.

When I met Antonio, he held the title of Vice President, Product Development & Creative Director for Radio Flyer. In this role he saved the company from going bankrupt. By the mid-nineties when Antonio came back to help, Radio Flyer had become a little too old fashioned. What started as a small quaint company selling its first wooden wagon in 1917 and run by the third generation of Passins, had over time become a stodgy, outdated manufacturing anachronism based in an old Chicago manufacturing plant. It had lost its competitive touch, didn't create cutting edge product, was not investing in marketing or conducting the necessary R&D that their larger competitors used to discover consumer preference for soft plastic wagons rather than steel ones that so easily rust during a long Midwest winter. Therefore they quickly saw their market share gobbled up by the competition (loosing more than 35% from the peak) and larger toy manufacturers like Mattel and Little Tykes began pushing them off the toy shelf and out of long held account relationships with retail partners such as Toys R US. Antonio's mission was to stop the bleeding and get Radio Flyer back into a market leadership position. And he did a great job. Within three years, he helped Radio Flyer increase sales by 30%, he developed 60 new products, representing 35% of total corporate revenues, and created the top five sellers for the company. He also broke into new toy categories including: miniatures, Christmas gifts, and collectibles.

The problem was, his string of business successes gave him a false sense of confidence that put him on a road that eventually led to my office. You see, when I met Antonio he had just spent the company's entire annul profits, about three million dollars, on an "all-in" bid to harness their brand to America's fascination with all things angelic. At the time there was a highly rated television show called *Touched By An Angel*, many books were being written about encounters with angels and it seamed that the time was right to build a toy that included a Radio Flyer wagon filled with little boy and girl angels. This led Antonio to create a brand new line called *Angel Love Wagon Babies* that he planned to promote via television advertisements. After writing a touching script that he said left the advertising executives at Bozell Worldwide in tears, he created the initial product designs and set up manufacturing in China, they ran the pilot commercial tests in St. Louis where the consumer response was flat. The simple fact was, the general public did not associate angels and little red wagons, and no matter how sweet the advertising copywriting was, public opinion was not going to change.

What I failed to mention in the telling of this story was that Antonio had done this all without telling his father, Radio Flyer's president. Antonio knew that his conservative father would veto the TV commercials and Antonio was just convinced in his heart that the company needed to move into the twenty-first century on the medium that big companies used to build brand awareness and capture consumer interest. So instead of consulting with dear old dad, he decided to take the initiative and later, when the orders would be flooding in, Antonio would explain what he had done.

Antonio, like Isaac, returned to the family business hoping to find that place where God would allow him to prosper. Like Isaac who reopened the wells that had been dug in the time of his father Abraham, which the Philistines had stopped up after Abraham died, Antonio began to rebuild a business that was "stopped-up." And for a season, the wellspring of success gushed out until adversity struck. In Isaac's case the herdsmen of Gerar quarreled with Isaac's herdsmen over the well, so Isaac left. In Antonios' case, his idealistic reach for success left him grasping a handful of failure and now he, like Isaac, had to leave the familiarity of the family business and dig again for God's blessing in his career.

CHAPTER III

DIGGING WELLS THROUGH ADVERSITY - ISAAC

STARTS TO DIG AGAIN.

By now Isaac is thinking, "if I just give away the last well we dug, the one I named Esek because of the dispute with the Philistine herdsmen, I'm sure they will leave us alone, after all they got what they wanted." But no, that didn't work either, after we dug another well and found fresh water, once again the herdsmen picked a fight with us and that led me to name it Sitnah which means opposition. How can it be that I go from Gerar where God blessed me more than I could have imagined in my wildest dreams to where I can't even find a place to water my flocks. But I won't give up, I'll get the men together and give them a pep talk. Remind them of God's goodness and his protection and his eternal promises. The pep talk was a piece of art. Here I am with 50 people whose very existence rests on my decisions and I hit a motivational homerun. Just to give you a taste of management 101, let me share with you the gist of the pep talk.

> "Gentlemen, we were brought here for a pur-
> pose and we were brought here by the living
> God. The God of my Father Abraham, my God
> and one day, the God of my son Jacob, we can't
> succumb to these wretched Philistine shepherds;
> we have as much right as they to care for our
> flocks and herds. We are the people of the liv-
> ing God. He is on our side and he will go be-
> fore us"

As a matter of fact, everyone was so pumped up that they hoisted me on their shoulders and started to sing and dance. Needless to say, digging another well with this much *esprit de corps*, was not going to be too hard to accomplish. And away we went to a good-looking place that was close by, but rather isolated, where no one seemed to be grazing, or for that matter, any signs of civilization even existed. In other words, it was the perfect spot. And the men began to dig. I thought it prudent to stay with them and spur them onward. We made a game of it. I offered two ewe for the one who could dig the longest and an entire ram for the first shovel to hit water. We dug all day, then we dug through most of the night under the bright lantern lights. We started digging all over again the next morning. We dug and dug and then we dug some more. Even I dug some, just to share camaraderie with the men. It was hard work but we were excited to see God work on our behalf. By the end of the third day we hit pay dirt. Oh what a beautiful sight it was. Water gushing, gurgling and bubbling out of the hot desert sand. Water, the elixir of life. We drank deep, we played in it and we splashed each other. Then we carefully watered the flocks and herds. Everyone was satisfied. We had finally done the hard work of digging our new well.

So you ask, "how did I know this was the right well?" Easy, no one fought with us over it. Matter of fact, I named it Rheoboth, for the Lord had made room for us. That very night, God came to me in a dream and reaffirmed his presence, protection and blessing in my life. The least I could do was build an alter right there to worship the living God.

Reader Takeaway -

Whereas it is in many ways much easier for non-believers to take risks and move in different directions, Christians tend to be somewhat fearful of losing a blessing, or frustrating God's will, or taking a wrong step thereby going against the leading of the Holy Spirit. Often we see God's will in a linear manner. Meaning once God plants us somewhere, potted we will stay. Sometimes we think our faith is best demonstrated by consistency and its reverse is instability. Thus, in the workaday world, if I hold my job for 25 years I am a faithful worker, and if I hold a job for only 2-3 years I'm unstable. That flies in the face of everything we experience in life as a Christian. Who of us can say I know exactly what my family, my life my living situation 2 years from now let alone 20 years from now. Digging another well is completely counterintuitive to the mainstream Christian who misinterprets the purpose of strife. Isaac shows us that strife was used by God to tell him to go a different way in order to find the peace of God. His faith in a loving God drove him to persist in continuing to dig another well even as each new well he dug was fought over. Isaac shows us that the battle of faith is the persistent pursuit of God in the face of adversity.

> Adversity is like the sand that Isaac had to dig through to get to the well water. Going through adversity deepens faith. The muscle we use to dig with is represented by persistent pursuit; the well represents a metaphorical conduit to

God's will. Sand is adversity to our faith, the shovel is our persistence.

When you persistently peruse God's will through the sands of adversity you will dig a conduit to the will of God. The Bible encourages us toward this goal in 1 John, chapter five; verse 14 – 15; "This is the confidence we have in approaching God: that if we ask anything according to his will, he hears us. And if we know that he hears us—whatever we ask—we know that we have what we asked of him."

It could be argued that our entire life as a believer is a means by which God deepens our faith through life experiences. His intention is not for us to reach complacent boredom or stagnation (for example, finding a job that we can hold for life) but rather to give us a dynamic adventure. The end result is a life spent hearing God's voice, responding to His will, persistently following Him and knowing He was faithful throughout each step in the journey of our faith. With the expectation that as we cross the great divide and are ushered into Heaven, we will hear from the Lord "well done, my good and faithful servant". But this life of adventure in faith, of persisting in the face of adversity and of trusting God to be a faithful Heavenly father is not the "simple Christian life". Unless we become familiar with the exercise of faith and recognize God's patterns, many of life's changes will appear as punishments, provocations and causes of despair – that's too bad.

The allegory of *Dig Another Well* attempts to show us that life is an adventure of pursuit. Isaac faithfully pursued God until God led him to himself. Life is full of dynamic change and change does not define God as ca-pricious. God remains the same but his believers need to adapt. Most people fear change and resist it whole-heartedly. That's also too bad. Because change is used by God to deepen our faith, bring out or enhance our gifts and talents as well as to bring us to Himself. I know God is saying; "Don't be afraid, I will never leave you nor forsake you." "I go to prepare a place for you."

When I speak of change, it is implied that your deci-sions need to be covered in prayer and should be con-firmed in the counsel of spiritual leaders, advisors and family. We can frustrate the will of God by saying "I made this career decision, because it is God's will" when in reality we did little or nothing to confirm whether it was or was not really God's will.

When Isaac finally reached the last well (which he called Rehoboth), the place without strife, God met him there personally. We Christians need to keep digging our wells, until we reach a point where God gives us peace. Because, as we see with Isaac's repeated efforts to dig another well, the end result is finding God's next step on your journey of faith. Which is the place where God meets us and abundantly provides for us.

Illustration – the day I received the call from Jimmy Cleamons in my Oak Park, Illinois office was a typical, early spring day, sunny and full of promise that Summer was just 'round the corner, but still on the cool side. When I head his voice, warm and gravely from many seasons of yelling out instruction to basketball players over the din of large arena crowds, I could not believe my ears. You see, Jimmy Cleamons was just about as famous as you could be in Chicago and not be named Michael Jordan.

When I moved to Chicago from Arizona after college, I like the rest of the population in Chi-Town became avid fans of the Chicago Bulls.   The first year I moved to the city, 1990, was one year before they won the first of their six championships. The Bulls players, their coaching staff and even ownership were considered royalty in Chicago and also provided the major distraction from the Windy City's blistering cold winters. Which I believe, if memory serves me, was one of the coldest on record that year.

By the time Jim called me to write his coaching philosophy and resume in order to pursue NCAA Division One head coaching opportunities, the following had occurred. The Bulls had won four of their eventual six NBA championships between 1991-1996, he had become the first African-American head coach for the Dallas Mavericks, then had been fired by the Mavericks, became the first and last head coach of ABL, Chicago Condors, a woman's team that folded in 1998, the same year it was founded, that is when I received his call.

If you schematically map out his work history, Jim had just gone through all three stages of a typical career path: career progress, career flat-line and career decline, and now in his late forties, wanted to go back to school and lead a college program. The only thing is, his last two head coaching jobs were failures and much of that was not necessarily due to his ability to lead or win, but rather too influences not clearly in his control.

In a way, the arc of Jim's coaching career and even his life, reflects that of Isaac. Both were early stars; Jim was Mr. Ohio in Basketball, Played four years for his favorite college team, Ohio State University, and went on to play for nine years in the NBA, a time that includes winning an NBA championship in 1973 with the LA Lakers. Isaac was also a star early in his life, he represented God's promise that Abraham would be the father of many nations; through Isaac we have Jacob who became Israel from which the entire Jewish race originates. When Isaac moved to Gerar, God increased him one hundredfold, making him one of the wealthiest men in what is now on the South border of Palestine. And at some point for both men, the good times stopped rolling which led each to start digging for a new well.

Since the middle part of "Dig Another Well" chronicles the struggle, strife and continuous well digging that Isaac had to go through to finally reach God's blessing, it is worth pointing out some facts that might go unnoticed about Jim's career.

Let's start with Dallas, a time that is equivalent to right after Isaac received a hundredfold blessing. When Jim took over the reins of the team, he owned four NBA championship rings, three as an assistant head coach and one as a player. He was a hot, hot commodity as a prospective head coach and if it hadn't been for the Bulls General Manager Jerry Krause refusing to grant Cleamons permission to talk with teams seeking new head coaches, or even let teams know if he'd be interested in their jobs, he might have evaluated more offers. But as it were, he decided on Dallas.

When I met Jim, I wanted to understand what had happened with the Mavericks, so I asked him bluntly, why were you let go so quickly. This is what I learned. In 1996 when the Mavericks initially approached Jim, they knew he had the pick of teams that had turned over their coaching staffs that year, so to make the deal sweet, they offered him the roles of General Manager and Coach. Nowadays that is somewhat a common request by the hot coaches in the NBA, but when this was offered to Jim it was still a pretty novel idea. Instead of grabbing the offer and the power that goes with both job titles, Jim requested that he focus on the team with one stipulation, that he be involved with the hiring decision of the next G.M. Of course this type of nuanced request is not put into a contract and although they assured Jimmy that he would have input, his opinion was never considered when the team selected Don Nelson as GM later that year.

What you might not understand about the selection of Don Nelson as GM is that it represented a very direct threat to Jim's ability to lead the team. In the NBA, the players tend to be managed oftentimes a little like herding cats, they tend to operate on their own wavelength. That is why teams pay so much for proven winners (e.g. Phil Jackson and Pat Riley) because the players respect their coaching records and history of winning championships. In Jim's case, he was a rookie head coach and his team just hired one of the most recognized and experienced ex-head coaches in the NBA as the team's G.M., thus undermining the legitimacy of Dallas' commitment to Jim's tenure as head coach. Imagine you are a star guard who was the best player on your high school team, college team, off-season AAU teams, etc. and Jim is telling you to work harder, practice longer and play games more intensely. If you have even the slightest lack of faith in this coach, then you tune him out and, voila, you have a team mutiny. Well guess what, Jim had a rough first season and was fired before the half-way point of the next, to be replaced by, guess who, Don Nelson who went on to coach the Mavericks from 1997-2005.

The lesson here is that strife can come from any angle. It can come, and usually does, right after you have your best professional season. Our job as believers is to trust God in the storm and to keep digging. That's what Jimmy Cleamons did. As a matter of fact, it wasn't long after our collaboration that Jim was hired as an assistant coach for the LA Lakers where he helped guide the team to three consecutive NBA Championships in 2000, 2001 and 2002 as well as an NBA Finals appearance in 2004. Jim can still be found on the sidelines where he has had the joy of motivating all-stars like Kobe Bryant and Shaquille O'Neal to reach their peak potential.

CHAPTER IV

LET'S GO DIGGING

Why don't we go dig up that blessing of a new career that honors your gifts and abilities and allows you to bloom professionally? When it comes to the desert that job seeking seems to represent, the first thing you need to dig with is a good resume. But not just any resume, no you cannot go dig up a wonderful new job with a tired, old, boring career story that puts people to sleep. You need a "wow" resume that makes people want to talk to you.

Now I have been writing resume for 18 years. To date I have written over 4,000 resumes, two books on resumes and numerous articles that cover the ways to make a resume stand out. So you can imagine that this is a subject that I could dig up quite a bit of dirt on. But I don't want to overwhelm you with too much information overload, so I will simplify the way to write the perfect resume by teaching you my CAR resume writing strategy. CAR stands for Challenge, Action & Result. What you need to do is find one or two cars in every job you held. A good rule of thumb is one CAR per every five years of employment. What I mean is that you should have an illustration from your work-life where you were given a task, or were part of team given a task that in some way was a challenge to meet. That by meeting that challenge with certain actions you and or the team were able to deliver a result.

Here are a couple examples of CARs for you to review.

C.A.R   **Example 1**   Retail Manager

He Said   Managed sales and service of "While you wait and watch transformation" remount services for consumers on location at jewelry retailers such as Marshall Field's, Dayton-Hudson, and Zale's 1100 stores.

We Said   **Challenge:** Optimizing 35 sales teams that conduct 10,000 jewelry remount shows a year at 2,000 U.S. retail stores.
Action: Created the first *Master Schedule* to track all shows, each team's traveling cycle, and their downtime in order to minimize conflicts.
Result: The new *Master Schedule* reduced average costs from $750/show to $500/show, which saved $2.5M per year.

This client was able to simplify a complex matrix of sales people going to thousands of events a year and by optimizing costs that his company paid to hold 10,000 jewelry remount shows per year he was able to save $2.5 million.

C.A.R.	**Example 2**	Database/Systems Administrator
	She Said	Write reports and create customized databases in order to provide people with the tools they need to do their jobs, utilizing Informix 4gl,SQL, and Microsoft Access. Analyzing data and ensure accuracy of information contained within the databases.
	We Said	**Challenge:** Helping founder sell Domino Pizza. **Action** Created all financial reports for VP Finance during the due diligence process of selling Domino's Pizza. **Result 1** Bain Capital was the eventual buyer for $1BB.

This client helped the founder of Dominos, Kevin Monaghan, sell his company for $1 billion in 1998. She also helped the company double its size internationally from 1,000 to 2,000 stores (which represented 33% of all Domino franchises).

CARS are little stories that tell who you are and wow potential interviewers. The key is to give specific examples that make you unique or better than your peers (an peer-to-peer comparison CAR is powerful). You can estimate figures, if you can't remember the exact numbers make a WAG (wild assumptive guess) just be conservative.

Think about the following - #, %, $, !
$ - How much money did your work earn for the company? How much revenue did your projects save the company? What is the value of accounts you serve? What were annual revenues or profits?

- Quantify your experience as best you can. How many people did you supervise or customers did you interact with daily? How many transactions were conducted?

% - Did you implement a program that improved something by a certain percent? Did profits, revenues, or sales increase? Did you save time (i.e. reduce a cycle of time commitment from 8 hours to 4 hours) with a process you created or redesigned?

! – What did you do that your supervisor would describe as exemplary? Was there something extraordinary about your work or your team? Did you break a record, set a new standard, or out-perform a prior year or another company?

GREAT COVER LETTERS

Next you need a good letter of introduction to comple-ment your newly created "wow" resume. I want to de-mystify the cover letter as one of the key elements of a successful job search and what I mean by "demystify" is that far too many people think that writing a concise, focused and compelling letter is a mystery, but it shouldn't be. Really the cover letter should be one of the easiest things you need to create to reach your dream job.

With that said, it doesn't mean that the cover letter can't be the star of the entire job search. Companies, like humans, tend to appreciate the fact that you admire them, that you know something salient about them and that you understand what makes them special. The problem is, if we use a staid, boring or un-interesting approach at wooing them, we can strike out just like the poor schmuck who uses cheesy pickup lines at the local dance club. In other words, we need to think differently and be unique.

The bulls-Eye cover letter is the answer to a question that every job seeker has, "How do I find a great job at a good company if my personal and professional network doesn't include someone that works at the target company I am interested in pursuing?" The answer is to use a "Targeted" cover letter.

BULLS-EYE COVER LETTER DEFINED
A cover letter composed from content gathered after you conduct company research online by reading press releases, newspaper articles, trade journal articles etc, that quote key decision makers, (those are also the hiring authorities such as

senior executives at the target companies) and writing a cover letter to these decision makers that refer to the research you conducted and where you tell them you want to be part of the initiative, rollout or project that is touted in the article, press release or newsletter.

Three Key Actions

①   Go to main library, *find a Business Reference Librarian* - ask him or her to help you locate the Online Business Databases and look for articles in a career area you are interested in targeting, i.e. sports marketing. Identify companies that specialize in your interest area.

Example   Sport Marketing job at IMG (world's largest sports marketing firm). Total research time = 15 minutes

②   Look for new directions the company is taking (i.e. IMG buys Clear Channel's event marketing firm, Live Entertainment to form IMG Live!)

- Get names of decision makers and send resumes to them. In this case they noted that Lee Heffernan will continue to manage the new IMG division. If you go to IMG Live! Website you will find Lee Heffernan's email address in the "who we are" section.

③   Write a cover letter that references something they were quoted as saying in the press release or article. Send resume and cover letter to target audience.

Example: Amanda Grouse

Amanda was a recent college graduate with a degree in marketing and wanted to pursue a career in corporate event planning. Like many new college graduates, Amanda sent a resume and standard cover letter to a variety of potential employers. But Amanda had her eye on working at the Ice Palace, which happens to be the home of the Tampa Bay Lighting, a premier NHL hockey team. Of course, Amanda did not have contacts at the Ice Palace so the letter she wrote was generic in form and content.

NOTE: Exactly what you are looking for during your research is **inexact**; the topics are only discovered during the research and rarely, if ever, pre-determined, you just need a nose for topical, interesting, trendy issues.

For the Ice Palace, the main issue Amanda discovered in a Google search turned out to be their status as a potential host for the 2004 Republican National Convention.

The article Amanda found on the Internet was as follows:

Tampa preens to sway

GOP's selection panel

Up against New York and New Orleans, Tampa must prove it can handle the convention.

By D. KARP, © St. Petersburg Times, published August 6, 2002

TAMPA -- The wining and dining begins tonight. The area's Republicans spent Monday finalizing elaborate plans to woo the delegation that will decide what city will host the 2004 Republican National Convention.

She then went directly to the main source, the Ice Palace home web site, www.icepalace.com and started reviewing recent press releases. This led her to uncover a news release quoting the VP of Public Relations who announced that the Ice Palace had been selected as one of four potential sites (ironically, they weren't the site that was eventually picked, that honor belongs to New York City). This bit of sleuthing, led Amanda to rewrite her cover letter with information reflecting her research that she then sent to the Director of Season Sales, two weeks after the first cover letter she had sent, with the cover letter reading as follows:

AMANDA'S *BULLS-EYE COVER LETTER*

Chad Johnson
Director of Season Sales
Ice Palace
401 Channelside Dr., Tampa, FL 33602

Dear Mr. Johnson:

Congratulations on being chosen as one of the potential venues to host the 2004 Republican National Convention! It must be a very exciting time for you and your company.

I know I could be beneficial to many departments in your organization, although my education and key interests lie in event planning and public relations. As you can see from the enclosed resume, I have had various leadership experiences including Greek Week Steering Committee and Senior Class Council. I always jump at the opportunity to take on a challenge.

I have held several jobs that allowed me to work directly with the public while serving and fulfilling the needs of guests and clients. A year-long internship within the public relations field afforded me invaluable experience and a great deal of knowledge, tam now interested in seeking a full-time job that will allow me to grow along with the company, both personally and professionally. My intense work ethic, enthusiastic attitude, strong self-motivation, and oral and written communication skills will prove valuable in contributing to the Ice Palace's strategies.

I'm not sure if or where you may need a new associate but I can assure you that I would make an outstanding team member. I hope you will consider my request for a personal interview to discuss further my qualifications.

I can be reached at (813) xxx-xxxx or by e-mail at amanda@aol.com. Thank you for your time and I hope to hear from you in the future.

Sincerely,
Amanda Graul

The result. Amanda won an interview and was hired as the Ice Palace's Suite Services Coordinator.

NOW WE NEED TO HUNT YOUR JOB

Finally we need to make sure that we have the right attitude about the job search. What I typically see are clients who are in some state of confusion regarding how to properly go about a smart job search. They are confused about where to send their resume, what company is best suited for them and their skills. They don't know if they will have to relocate or take a salary cut. Whether they will like their new boss, co-workers or even the physical environment of the new work place. All this confusion leads to paralysis.

So what do you do about all your questions? Ignore them. The fact of the matter is that a job search is a process of discovery, not of knowing. That is an exciting prospect, you don't quite know what fish will bite your bait, but some company has a piece of puzzle missing that you fit, it is just up to us to get our puzzle piece out to as many corporate puzzles as we can so that we get interviews.

Think of it this way. Isaac did not know where he was supposed to dig his new well, just that he had to dig. You don't need to know who is going to hire you, just that you need to look. After working with 4,000 clients one thing I have learned is that after a little probing, every client has some idea where they should dig. But there is a little bit of comfort in over-analyzing our situation because that keeps us from having to do the hard work of digging (it also protects us from potential rejection). But Isaac shows us that even though his digging initially led to Esek (strive) and Sitnah (struggle) he eventually found Rehoboth (room) and the peace of God.

FOOT LICKERS IN INDIA

What can keep you from finding your own Rehoboth is getting "cold-feet". Cold feet come from an imaginative mind that conjures up all the negative possibilities and that leads them not to send their resume out to as many opportunities that they can find. That's too bad. What I tell my clients is if they send out their resume and get a call from a company looking for foot lickers in India, they need to show some sort of interest in the opening. A lack of interest in a job opening to the interviewer is the kiss of death. So don't shoot yourself in the foot when you are called for a job that on the front-end doesn't seem palatable. You will be amazed how that can change if you interview excellently and impress them well enough that they may see you as a good fit for a job that you might like.

A great example of this principle in action is a client of mine named Dan Swartz. Dan is an Information Technology (IT) professional whom I have helped three times in the past. Each time we worked together he would hire me to write his resume, cover letter and then have me send it out to 400-500 executive recruiters I have in a database that specialize in IT. During our third collaboration it occurred to me that Dan was sabotaging the efforts when the recruiter called-back because he was inflexible regarding relocating. The problem was that Dan had two children in high school in one of the most prestigious suburbs in Chicago, Naperville (Naperville Central high school is among the top 3 percent in the nation in a U.S. News and World Report survey) and Dan was not about to relocate until after they graduated. So what would happen is that a recruiter would call and as soon as Dan sensed they might expect him to relocate (which usually took him less than two minutes to discern) he would thank them for the call and politely explain his situation then get off the phone. That meant he didn't turn these cold calls into warm relations. He felt he was being polite and not wasting the recruiter's time, I felt he was missing a golden opportunity. That's when I explained the "Foot Lickers in India" analogy. What happened next? Dan called me two days latter to share a conversation that he had just had with a recruiter. The call started with the woman mentioning that they were looking for an IT manager in Santa Fe, New Mexico and the job paid $75,000 per year (at the time Dan was earning over $120,000). This is the exact type of call Dan would have historically cut short, of course politely, but without attempting to build rapport. This time he remembered my admonishment to sound interested (even on the front end this appeared to be a dead end) and try to turn this recruiter into a long-term partner for his career. Well a funny thing happened. Thirty two minutes into the call (you see Dan, being a tech geek with a digital watch was timing the conversation) the lady finally noticed his early career working for the commodity markets in Chicago (the Chicago

Board of Trade and the Mercantile Exchange). That is when she mentioned that they had clients in Chicago in the financial markets and that those positions paid well into six-figures, more like what he wanted to earn. The point is that by remaining interested even in a job he no interest in taking initially, led to a dialog about a job that fit him perfectly. This possibility would never have opened had Dan defaulted to his traditional approach.

Suzy Q's Doughnut Hut vs. IBM

The other time many people get cold-feet are at the actual face-to-face interviews. That's because many job seekers rightfully send out hundreds of resumes to just about anything that might appeal or fit their career profile. Let's say one resume goes to IBM and another to Suzy's Doughnut Hut. Sure enough Suzy's calls first. Being the dutiful applicant you go on that interview albeit, reluctantly. You might be thinking, well I can practice with Suzy and wait for that re-al job at IBM to call me. Sure enough in the inter-view you don't really try to win an offer. In other words you are lackadaisical, disinterested and maybe a little aloof. Of course, Suzy can tell that you are not excited about the job and the interview becomes a formality. You chalk it up to practice; I chalk it up to "cold feet".

Remember the only goal of the interview is to win an offer. You can turn down an offer, negotiate it or leverage it against other offers. If you predetermine that Suzy's Doughnut Hut is wrong and justify that assumption by thinking about your real interest in IBM, then you sabotage your own efforts. Without really trying to do everything in your power to win

the offer, you are just wasting her and your time.
Don't do that.

THE FINAL EQUATION

When all the dust settles and you are in the midst of
the job search the bottom line is that searching for a
new job is equivalent to *seeking* God's will (always a
good thing) but accepting a job offer means you are
acting on God's will. The difference between seeking and acting on God's will is an important distinc-
tion to make. Because Christians tend to get the two
mixed up, job search paralysis can easily set in. The
reason we are confused about the difference is that
seeking requires action so it appears to be the same as
acting on God's will. But it isn't the same. Think of
it this way, if you were single man hoping to find a
wife it would be necessary to do those things associ-

ated with seeking, i.e. going out to dinner, socializing, going to a movie with a prospect or two. But until you ask someone to marry you all these pre-proposal activities can be lumped into seeking God's will for a spouse. Once the man makes a proposal, then you are acting on God's will. What is the difference here, seeking God's will does not change your life or personal situation, but acting on God's will does. In this example, once the proposal is accepted you are now engaged, which is much different that not being engaged. Acting on God's will always changes your life, whereas seeking does not. Here is another example. Let's say that you no longer want to live in Chicago but feel that God might very well like you to relocate. But you know that you are active in your church, your kids are happy in their school and you enjoy your neighborhood, so you just dismiss the idea out of hand. That is like putting God in a box. We usually justify ignoring the holy spirit's leading by conducting some kind of pro and con analysis, pitting the reasons for and those against in some kind of list that eventually leads us to make our own decisions, quite often apart from God's will. What if you said instead, maybe God does want me to move even if I am flourishing here, why don't I just look where he might want me to move. In this case say to California. What do you have to do to seek his will? Will buy plane tickets, book a hotel, rent a car and go to California and look at homes or apartments. In all of these activities your life does not change, this is what I call seeking God's will. Now if you buy a house or sign a lease then you are acting on God's will. I believe that we should always be seeking his will, but that acting on his will requires strong prayers, the counsel of many and agreement of those who are important, i.e. wife or parents or mentors, etc.

Careers are like this. Just because you are sending out your resume and even having phone or face-to-face interviews does not mean you will leave your present job. Only when you accept an offer, i.e. act of God's will, does your life change. So we should always be seeking, but acting requires prayer and counsel. Don't get confused on this point. That means you should send your resume to all kinds of jobs in all kinds of locations and let God direct your path to his Rehoboth (place of peace) in your life.

EPILOGUE
Why I Became A "Master Digger"

As promised in the prolog, here are a few of the wells I've dug since starting on this journey to bring career advice to Christians.

After the Midday Connection appearance in 2004, I thought that Moody radio would love to have an ongoing Christian career coach give advice periodically. Unfortunately, I was not a 501 3(c), meaning I was not a non-profit and thus would be a conflict to Moody's status with the IRS. Of course as I kept writing inquiries to Wayne Petersen (the station manager), I did not know this was important until the seventh email finally prompted Wayne to call me and ask if I was formally designated as a non-profit. Which led me to my next well, God's Job.org, an official non-profit.

Wayne graciously allowed me to create two short format spots on "singles in the workplace" and "mothers returning to work," but neither seemed to address my desire to coach believers through the battleground of the job search and I left that well for another day.

My next effort was to solicit 650 radio stations on the idea of a talk show with a live career coach. The response was a loud "no thank you." So I narrowed my pursuit to the National Religious Broadcasting (NRB) radio station members. I was after all, now an official non-profit, right. This led me to fly Chris Wright (a senior engineer of Moody Radio), my wife and I to the 2004 NRB show in Anaheim, California to pitch radio stations on the idea of Christian Careers In Action, aka the Christian CIA. With Chris being an actual living and working employee of Moody, I thought we might now have the legitimacy to win station favor. Unfortunately, the stations do not gather in an identifiable way so we had a very hard time pitching them. But it didn't take long to see that the national broadcast companies had large hospitality suites in the adjacent hotel. That led me to the Salem Radio Network (SRN) suite.

SRN in 2004 was the 800-pound gorilla of Christian broadcasting. They owned nearly 100 stations and had affiliation partnerships with as many as 600 other outlets. They were also a publicly held company. So they understood the need for reaching profitability. An important point because many in the Christian community had no interest in a ministry that focused on careers, salaries and professional advancement. When I first approached SRN on the second day of this three-day convention, I met a lovely account executive who explained to me how SRN's XM Radio Channel 170 could use my program as a tool to sign up employers wanting to advertise job openings to a national audience. Which was perfect. I didn't know how to sell advertising space, but I did know how to coach Christians on conducting a job search.

This all changed when I met with the VP of Operations and learned about their "Pay to Play" approach. In this scenario, I would pay SRN $1,500 per week to buy an hour on their XM channel that would run from 1-2 pm on Saturdays. Talk about a quick change of plans. First they are going to use me as an advertising platform, next they are going to charge me to build a show. But I was willing to give it a try, thinking that I only needed a few clients per week to break even. So on the first weekend in June, 2005, I set up my Comrex Unit, put on my headphones and started broadcasting the Christian CIA across the nation. For the next 16 weeks I produced a live show broadcast each Saturday and I would have broadcast longer, but I ran out of money. While digging this well, I learned two important lessons. First, the audience for XM in 2005 on Saturday afternoons was largely made up of long-haul truck drivers and although I enjoyed them calling in to discuss how they might get back to their early careers, there simply weren't enough of them to keep the show alive. Secondly, I learned that "pay to play" was an easy way to go broke.

Although this was a setback and an expensive lesson, I wasn't deterred. You see, just before we signed with SRN to do the radio program I had just inked my first book deal. That entailed not only my digging but also my wife digging a new well.

Ever since I started writing resumes in 1991, I had kept all my client's "before" resumes to compare with the "after" resume that I would compose for them. I thought that this would be a good way to convince a new client to hire me to write their resume. Over the years from 1991 to 2001, I had collected a couple thousand examples and wanted to write a book on resumes. The thing is, publishers are only interested in unique book proposals and resume books were not unique, so finding an interested publisher was not easy. Lo and behold in walks in one of my clients whose boyfriend's mother just happened to work at McGraw Hill. After a quick email to my client's boyfriend's mother I learned of a senior publisher who I could contact using the mother's name as way of introduction. This led me to another person in the company and another and another until I finally met an editor who accepted my manuscript (and yes I had a completed manuscript available).

Over the next six weeks, I worked with this editor until

I got the phone call that terminated the relationship.

The call went something like this. "Robert, I just had a

meeting with the suits upstairs and was told to kill all of

my resume writing projects which includes yours."

"I'm sorry." So I was again at square one with my

book and frankly, I had absolutely no idea where to go

next. That is until my wife heard that the book industry

was going to hold their annual convention, the Book

Exposition of America (BEA) in Chicago the following

month and she thought she might be able to meet a lit-

erary agent who could shop our book for us. Well an

odd thing happened at the BEA, Marisa never met an

agent, but she did land two offers. The first one, and

the one I signed with, came from Ten Speed Press

where I was handpicked the founder and CEO, Phil

Woods. On the day I met Phil, he hand wrote the commitment to sign me, which I thought quaint (of course the faxed 12 page contract came later). During our first meeting, he verbally promised to publish two more books (on interviewing techniques and salary negotiation skills) because his stallion, Richard Bolles (What Color's Your Parachute?) was in his seventies and had implied that he was about to retire. Phil wanted a replacement available and thought I could be his new career guy. So I turned down a competitive bid from the second largest career publisher, Adams Media (they are known for the "Knock 'Em Dead", series by Martin Yates). But a funny thing happened on the way to the writer's hall of fame, although my first book "The World's Greatest Resumes" was picked as the Best 5 career books of 2005 by the L.A. Times, Ten Speed put zero marketing dollars and only sold 15,000 copies.

Richard Bolles never retired, his son began co-authoring the annual update of "What Color's Your Parachute" and I fell through the cracks.

But I never gave up digging new wells and since you are currently holding this book, God has led me to my new publisher and here I feel they have made room for me.

Romans 8:28

And we know that in all things God works for the good of those who love him, who have been called according to his purpose.

CONCLUSION

There are a million ways to dig another well and each of us need to connect with God to learn what, where and how to dig in agreement with his will for us. The resonating theme of life is that God is good and He doesn't change. Change is something for us to do in response to the call to love God, build our faith in Him and walk in His will for our life. Don't allow your circumstances to dictate your future or to diminish your faith in a loving heavenly father who gave everything to have a relationship with you.

If you are one of the 15.2% of the unemployed, underemployed or too discouraged to look for work population or simply feel stuck in a position that seems to be a dead end, or perhaps you are working for a company

that you have begun to see the "writing on the wall",
remember these key lessons from Isaac.

One   God's promise is eternal. No mater what our current situation is, the end of our story is secure and in a twinkling of an eye we will be with Him and every tear will be wiped away.

Two   Digging for God's will is a direct act of faith and the garden where faith grows best is often fertilized with strife and struggle. Don't forget that in the midst of every storm is a still small voice that reassures us…I love you, you are mine and I am here with you…

Three   There is a Rehoboth (place of room)

made for every person, a special job

waiting where your talents will bloom to

the glory of God. Isaac just kept digging

until no one fought with him anymore

and there God met with him once again

and renewed his covenant.

ABOUT THE AUTHOR

Robert Meier is a born-again Christian and employment expert. He built the largest career coaching practice in Chicago between 1991-2005, when he relocated his business to Florida. Since moving to Florida, he has authored three more career books and begun numerous effective career centers for faith-based organizations, universities, and labor-focused institutions (such as Workforce One and the Florida Department of Vocational Rehabilitation) and The JOYFM Christian Radio Station. He has advised the Congressional Committee on Education & the Workforce, has his career tools on the Department of Labor national career website, been featured on CNBC, Forbes, Fast-Company, Monster Careers and Fox News.

Coach Rob's overriding burden is to show men and women of faith how to uncover God's gifts and talents in their lives. His goal is to help work-seekers shine so that employers can appreciate the luster of their careers and then decide to add these jewels to their own corporate crowns of glory.

Robert resides in Clearwater, Florida with his wife Marisa and five children Arielle 16, Colten 13, Calais11, Trinity 9 and Rachel 7.

OUR MISSION: Healthy faith, healthy families and healthy careers are all important to God. Therefore, our mission is to equip men and women of faith to thrive professionally and reach God's destiny for their career.

To contact Robert:
prestojob@gmail.com
www.jobmarketexperts.org
www.fastrackjobs.org
Phone: 727-458-2690